This book belongs to

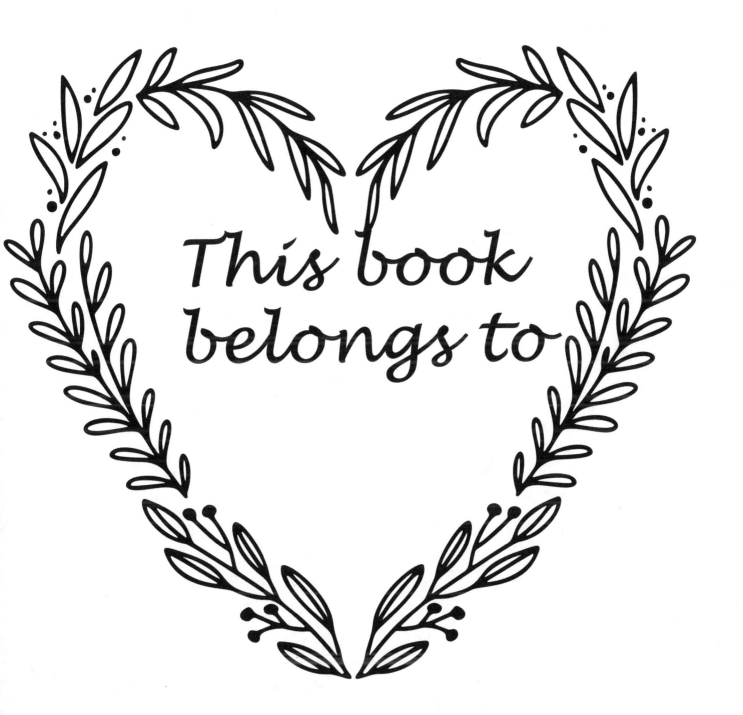

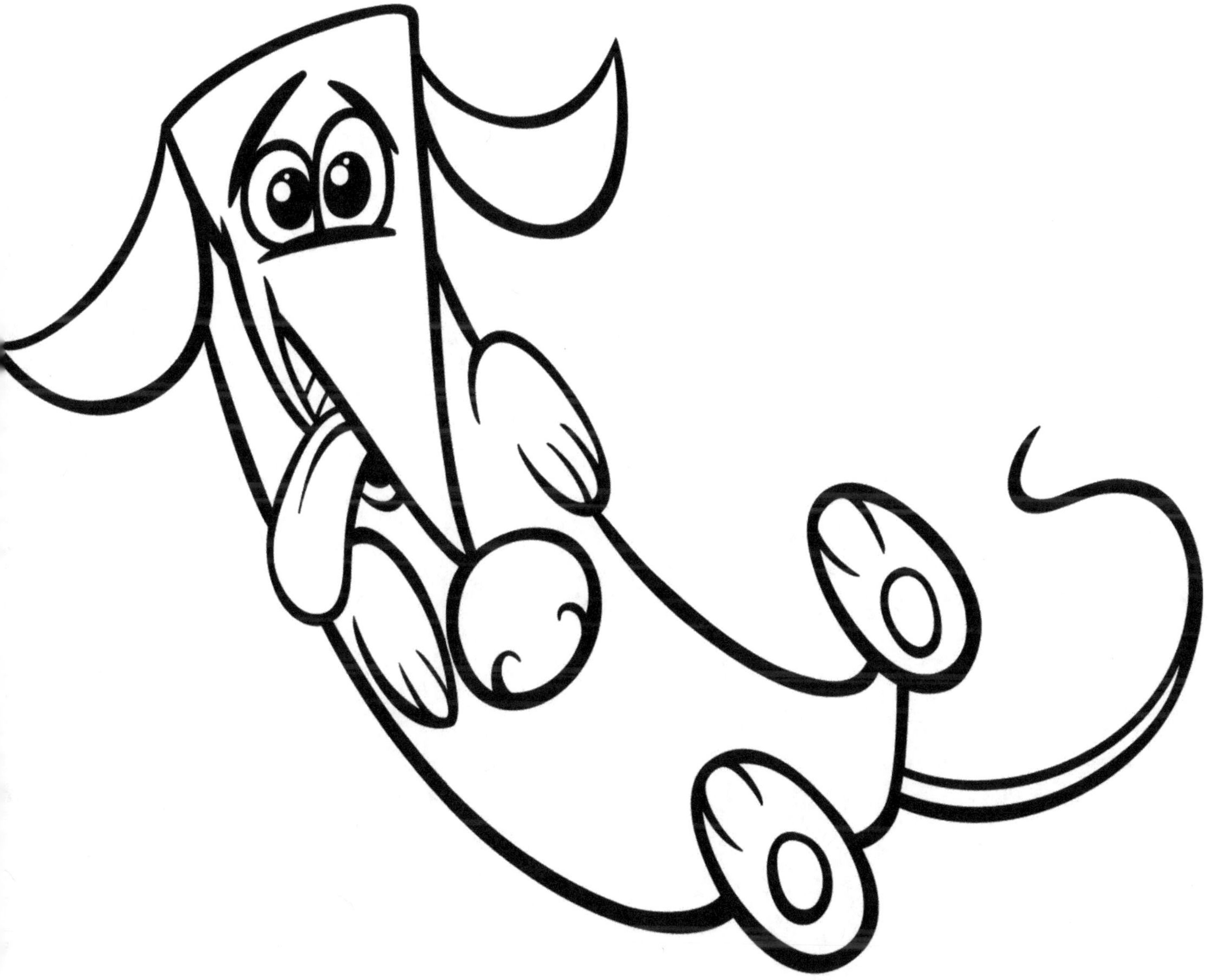

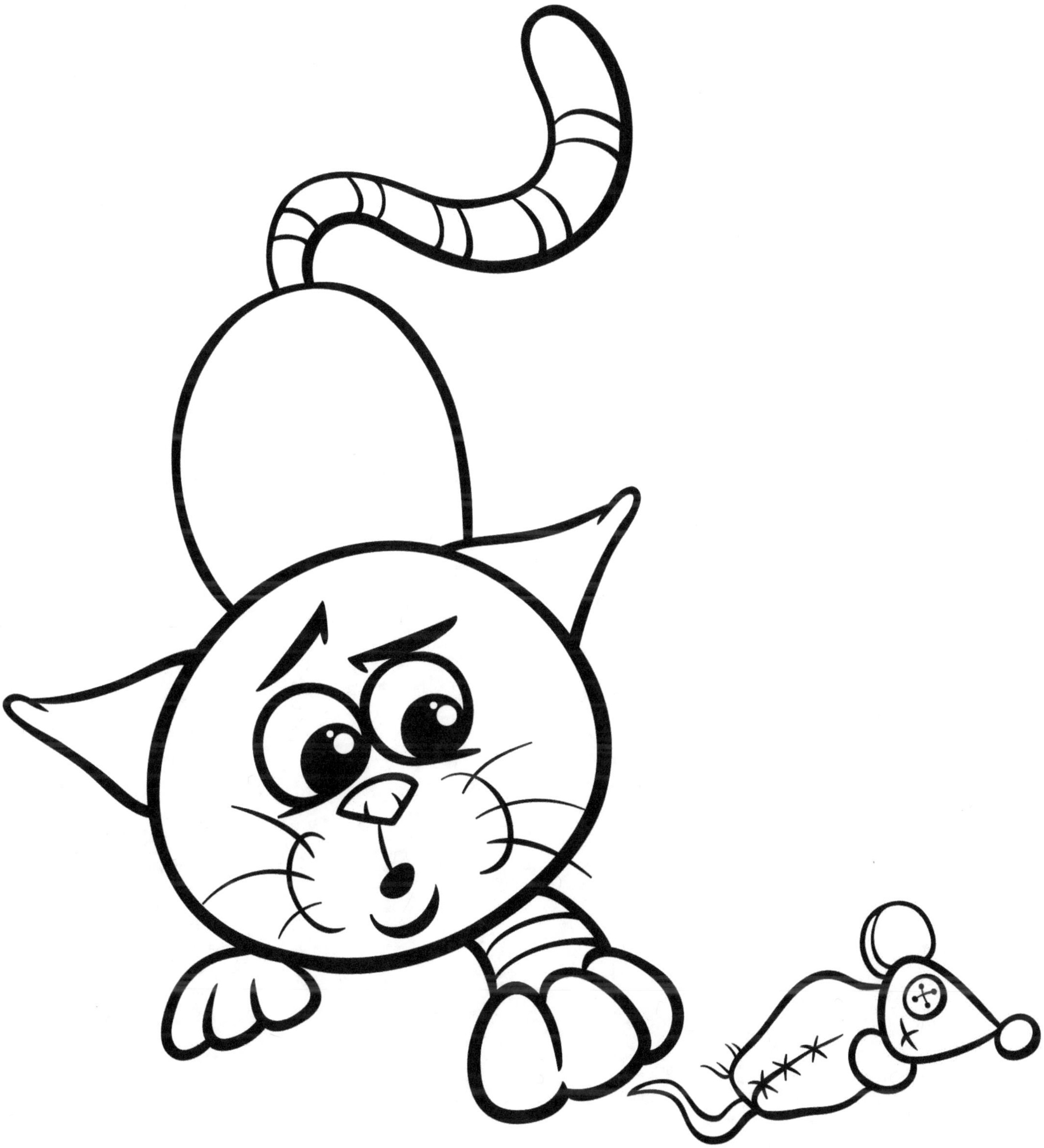

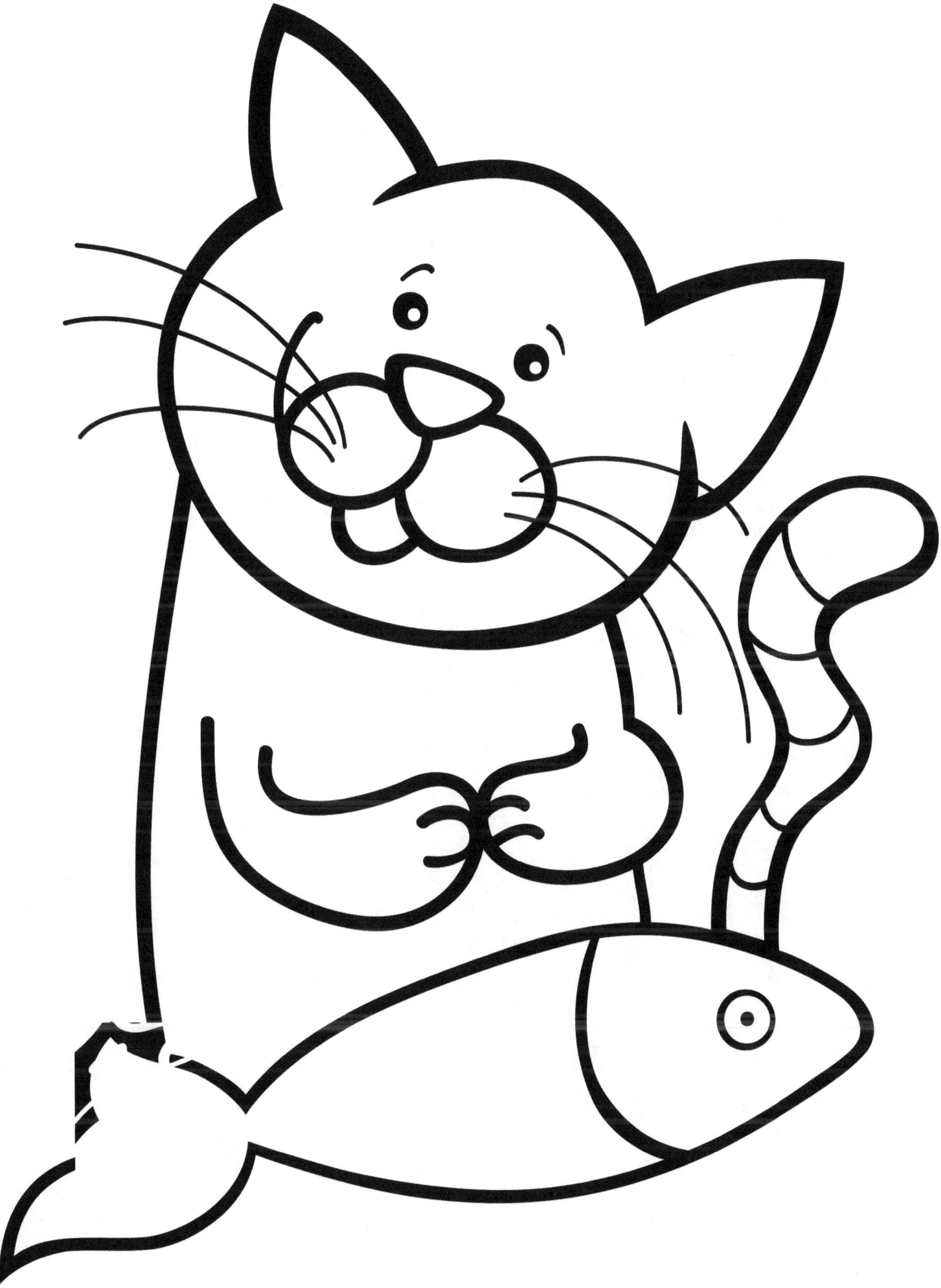

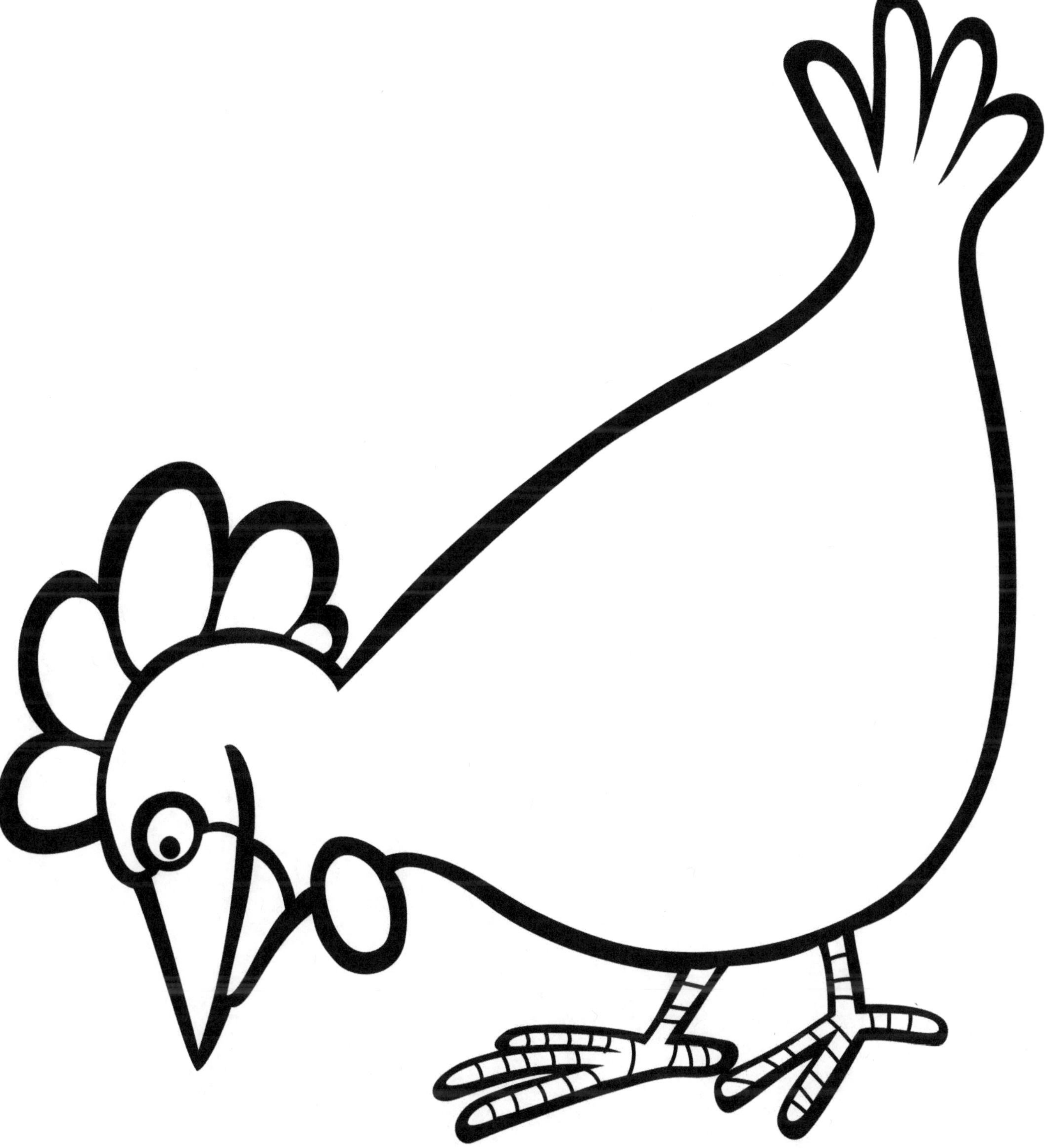

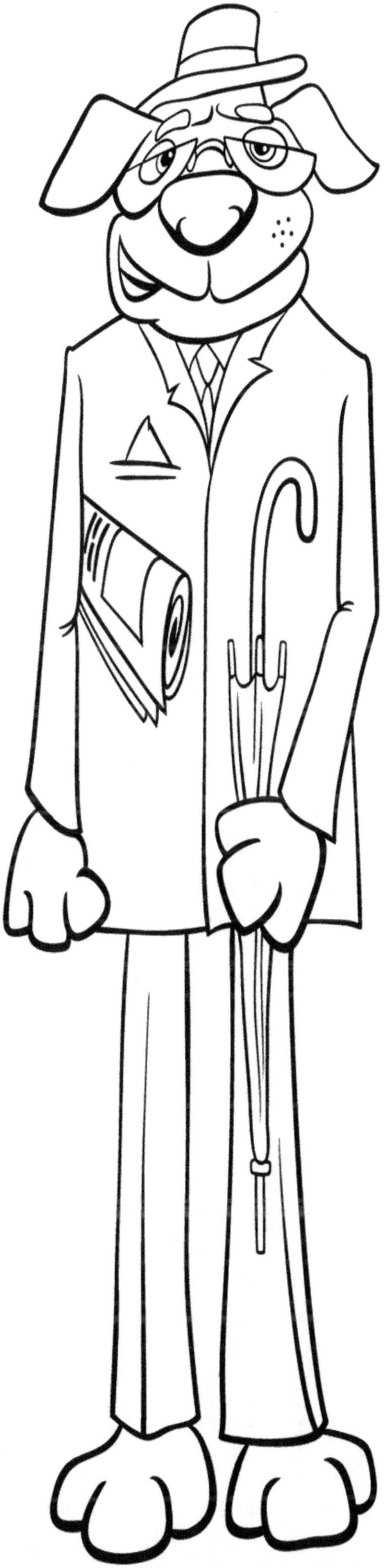

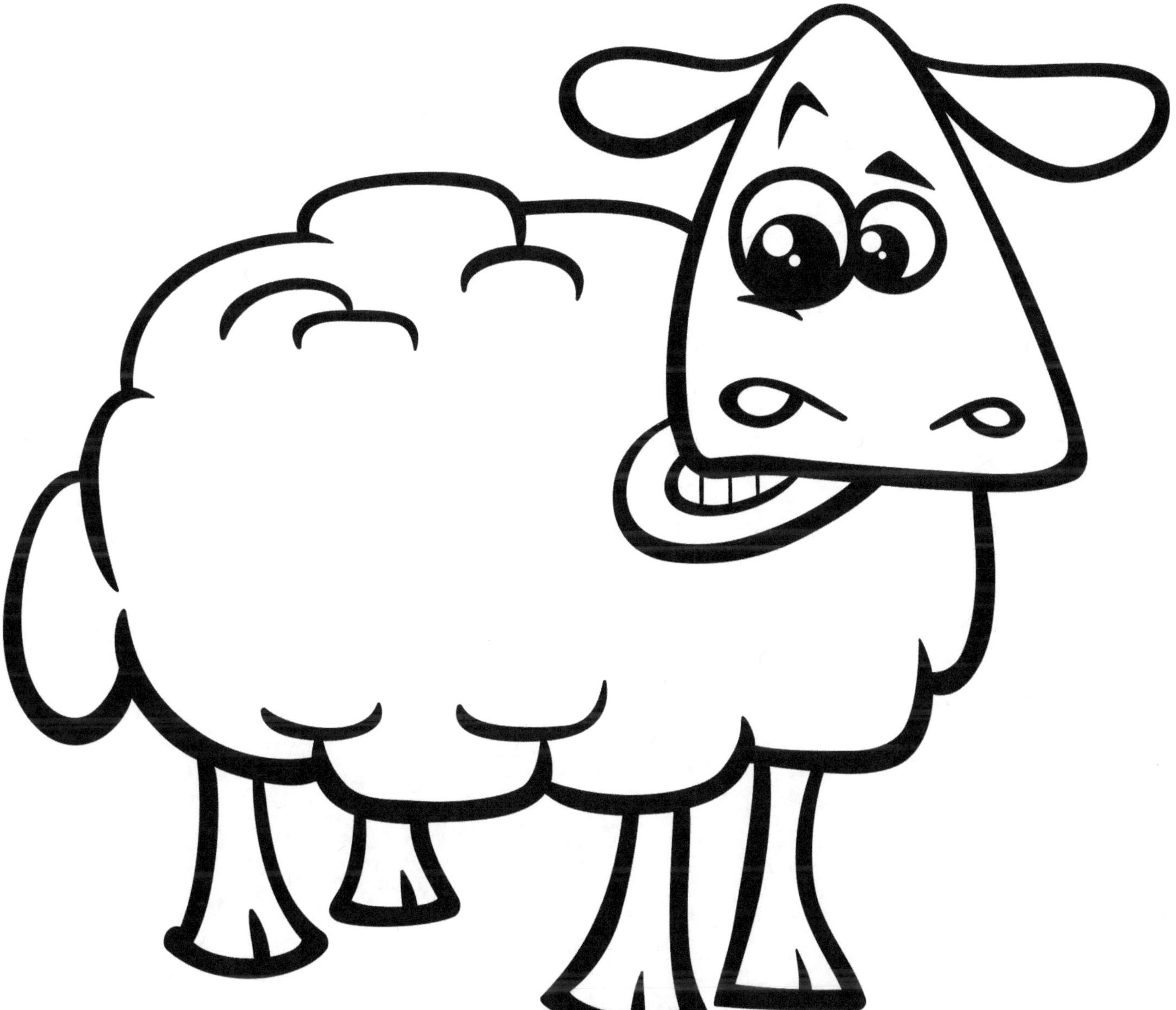

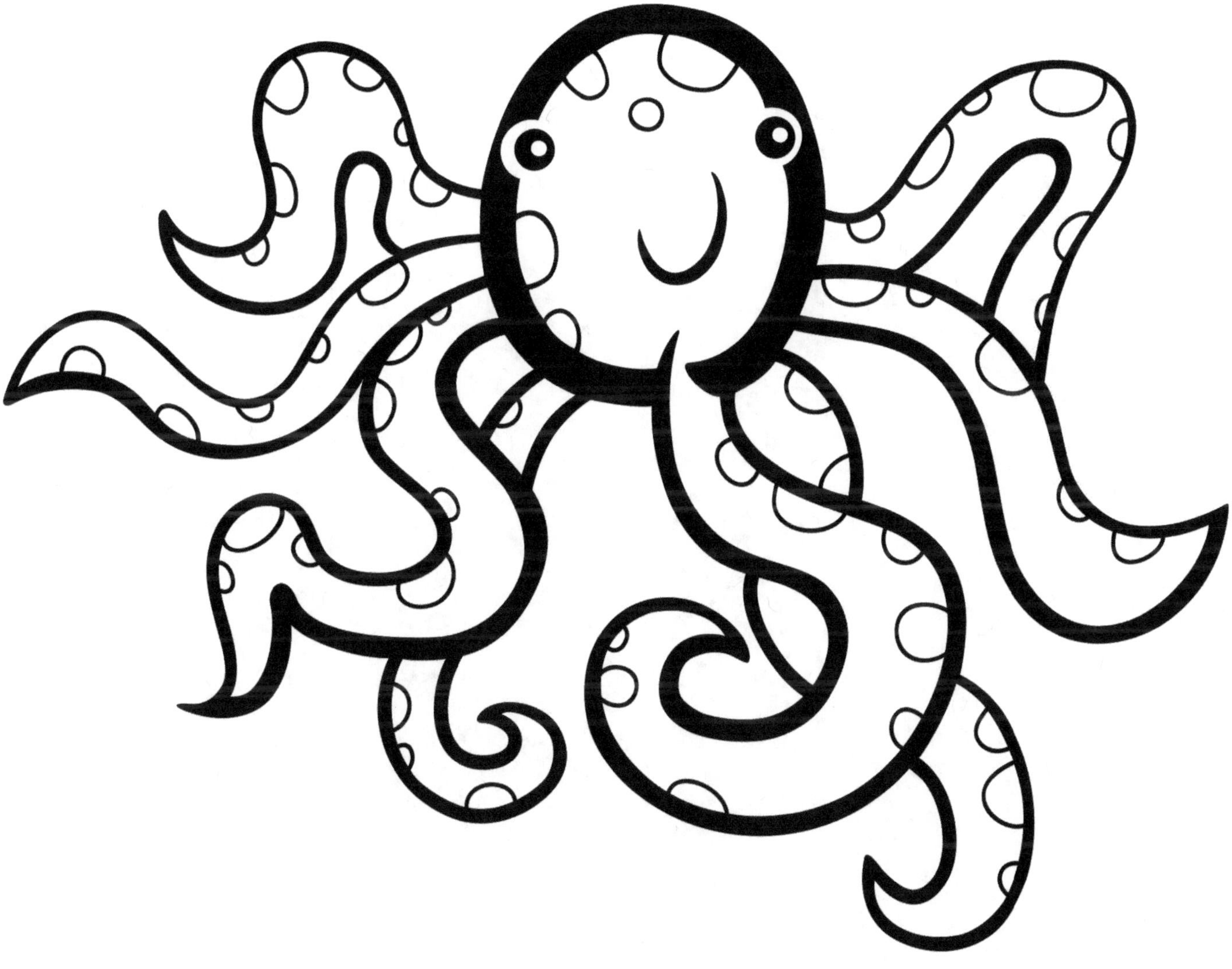

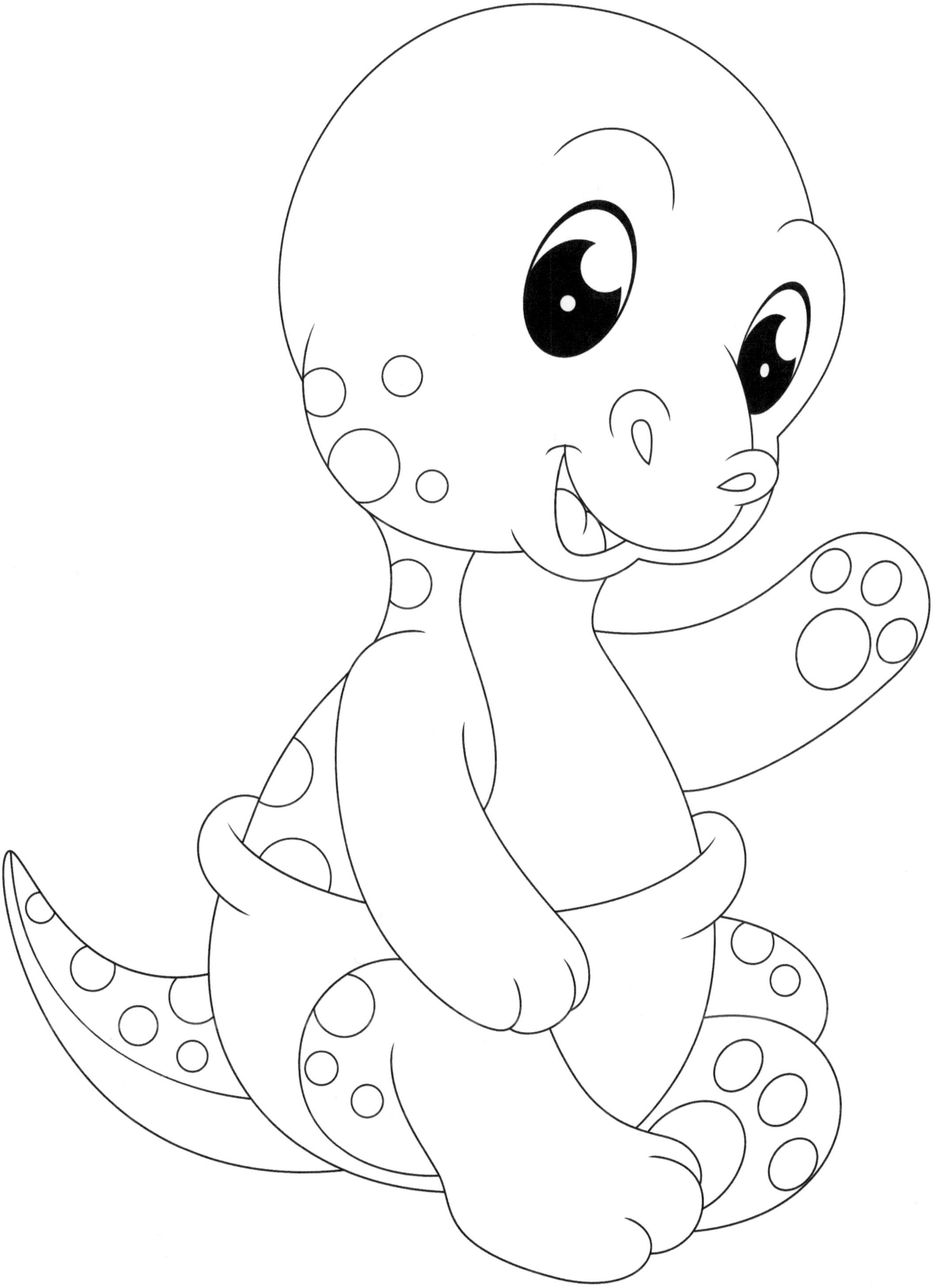

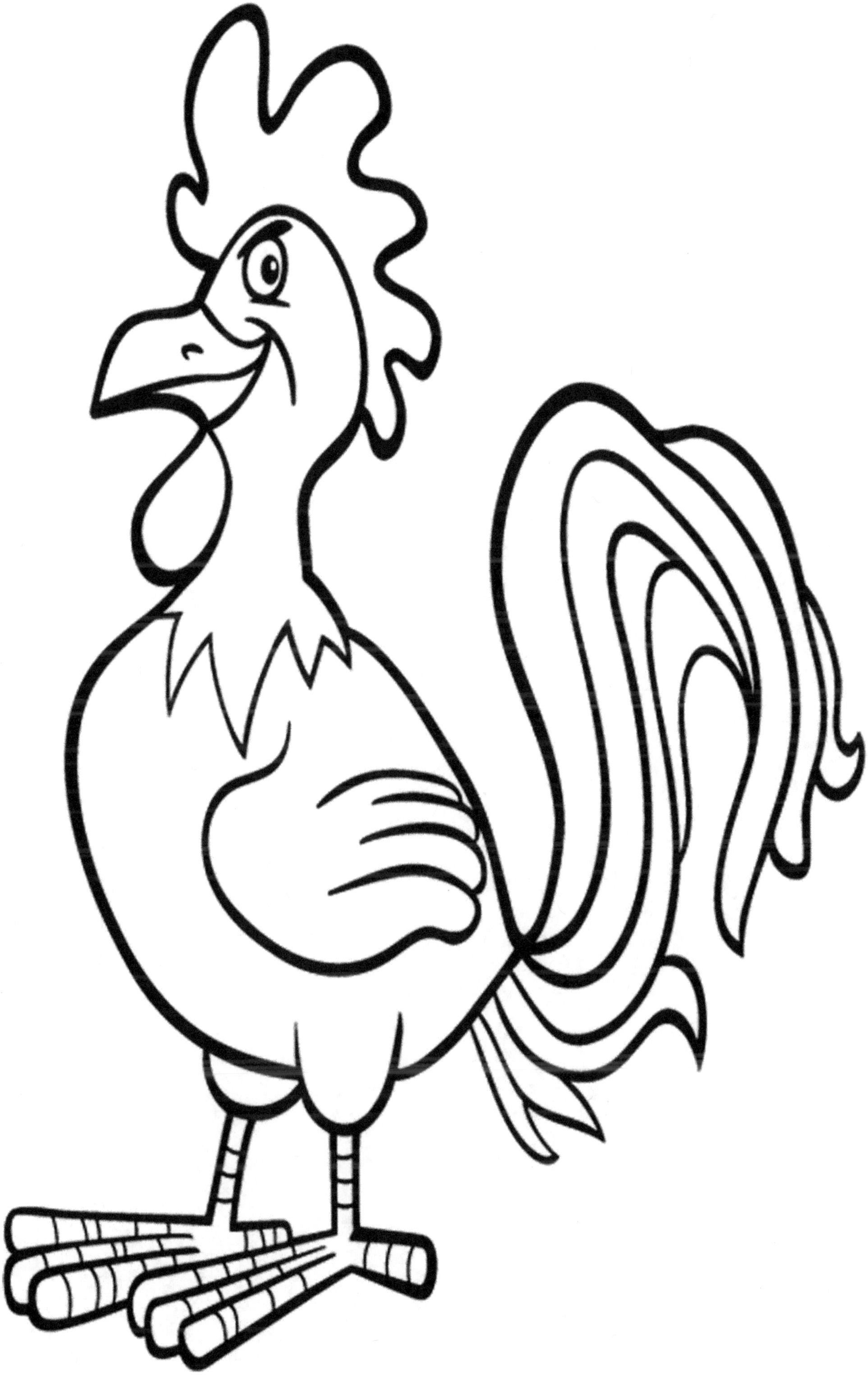

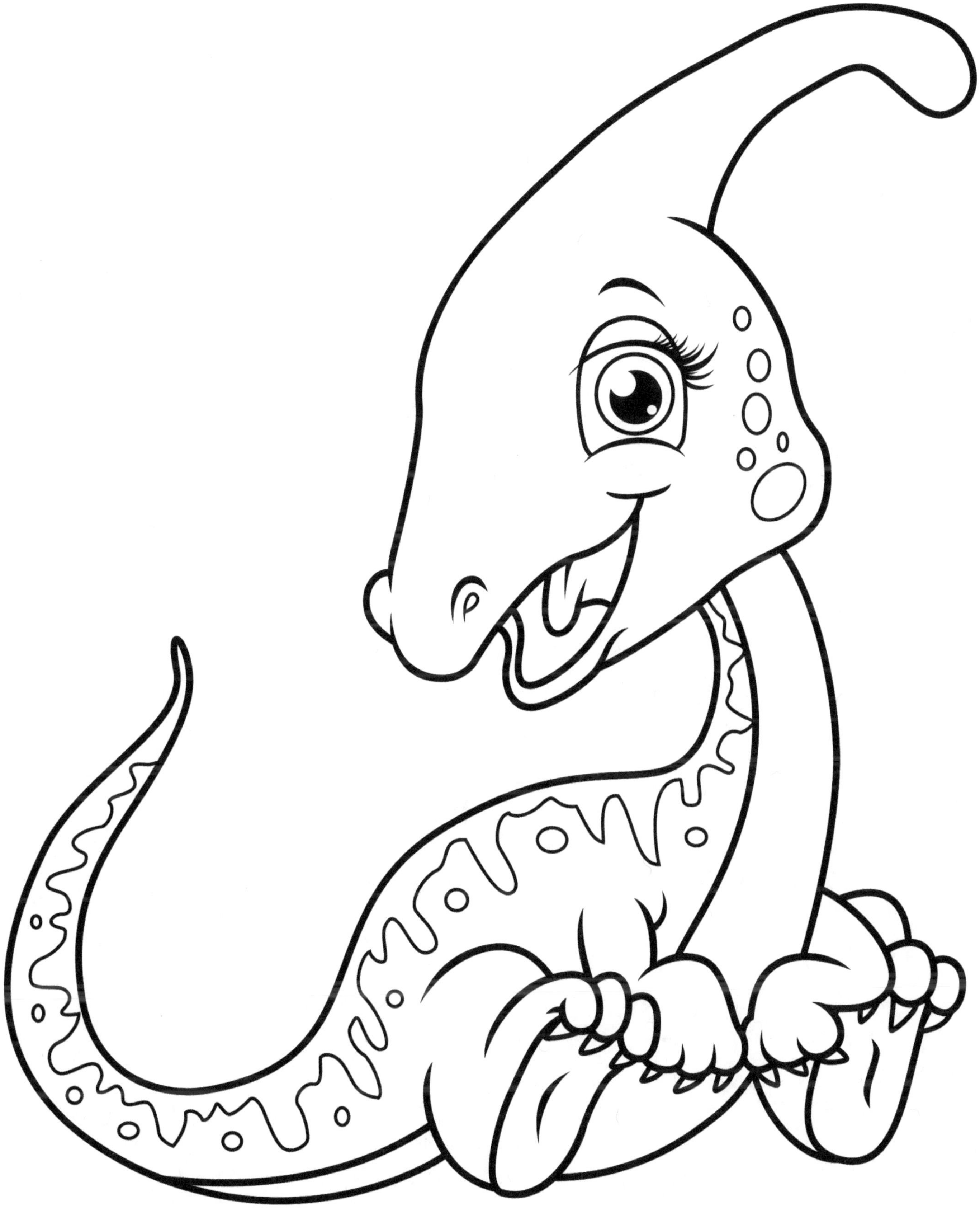

www.ingramcontent.com/pod-product-compliance
Lightning Source LLC
LaVergne TN
LVHW081800050326
832903LV00027B/2031
* 9 7 8 1 6 7 1 3 4 1 3 4 0 *